Finding the Right Spot

To Rick, always in my heart — JL

This one's for Terese,
for all of your loving encouragement — WM

Published by
MAGINATION PRESS
An Educational Publishing Foundation Book
American Psychological Association
750 First Street, NE
Washington, DC 20002

For more information about our books, including a complete catalog, please write to us, call 1-800-374-2721, or visit our website at www.maginationpress.com.

Editor: Darcie Conner Johnston
Art Director: Susan K. White
The text type is Times
Printed by Phoenix Color

Library of Congress Cataloging-in-Publication Data

Levy, Janice.
Finding the right spot : when kids can't live with their parents / by Janice Levy ;
illustrated by Whitney Martin.
p.   cm.
Summary: A young girl living with her foster parent describes the emotional ups and downs of being separated from her mother and living in unfamiliar surroundings.
ISBN 1-59147-073-0 (alk. paper) — ISBN 1-59147-074-9 (pbk. : alk. paper)
1. Foster parents — Juvenile literature. 2. Foster children — Juvenile literature.
[1. Foster home care.] I. Martin, Whitney, 1968- ill. II. Title.

HQ759.7.L48 2003
306.874—dc22   2003020675

Manufactured in the United States of America
10 9 8 7 6 5 4 3 2 1

FINDING THE RIGHT SPOT

When Kids Can't Live
With Their Parents

written by Janice Levy
illustrated by Whitney Martin

MAGINATION PRESS • WASHINGTON, DC

"**I** can so eat peanut butter three times a day," I told the family court judge, "and for your information, I love peanut butter more than anything in the whole world, except for my mom."

I told the social worker that the shelter me and mom lived in wasn't so bad, that after awhile you got used to all the noise, and the people who talked to themselves – well, those people you learned to leave alone.

Besides, living in a shelter taught you how to share stuff, like your food and things, and also how to hold on to what's really important and be thankful for what you've got 'cause there's always somebody worse off than you, and see, staying there with my mom, I was learning all the time.

"Why aren't you going to school every day and learning there?" the judge asked.

Well, I didn't have an answer for that.

She did.

So now I'm going to school and living with Aunt Dane.

She's not my real aunt, but says she loves me as if she was. Aunt Dane takes care of kids like me, when their real parents can't. Like when your mom loses her job and can't pay the rent for the apartment and drinks too much and gets sick so you stay home from school to take care of her.

That's what happened to me.

The judge sent my mom to a place to help her quit drinking. Then she'll get a good job and find us a nice place to live.

"Soon as I get back on my feet, I'll come get you," mom said. "We'll go out west and live on a ranch with horses. I'll open up a beauty shop. I love you, Cowgirl. Always and forever."

Sometimes mom visits me. We sit on the porch swing and eat peanut butter sandwiches and she does my hair up fancy like a movie star. I show her the pictures I've drawn of cactus and weathervanes and black stallions – mine is named Felicity.

Mom leans her head on me and gets all dreamy. "I can just about smell those horses," she says.

But sometimes mom's voice sounds wobbly on the phone and she laughs all the time or not at all.

I can hear her smoking and yawning and tapping her fingernails.

Her stories don't make sense.

On those days, she doesn't mention the ranch.

On those days, she doesn't come to visit.

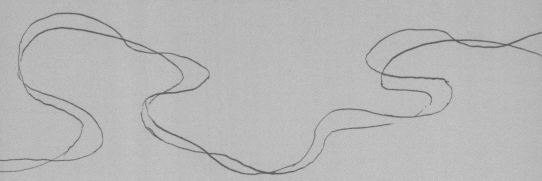

"It's not your fault," Aunt Dane says.
"Life just isn't fair sometimes."

She says she thinks there's a pot of gold at the end
of the rainbow or at least gumdrop trees, and
anyway things are gonna get better she just knows,
and in the meantime let's make some pizza?
So we mix the dough, and 'cause I'm so mad at
my mom I pound it until the whole house shakes.

"It's okay for you to cry," she says.

But mostly I hold it in.

I stare out the window and wonder what it would be like to live here forever where it's warm and safe and things come out of the oven when they're supposed to. Then I wonder how my mom would feel if she heard what I was thinking, so I make sure the window's shut good and tight, even though I know it's silly, so my thoughts won't slip out.

But I have to fling open the window and take a deep breath, letting the cool air whoosh against my face. Aunt Dane is nice and I like it here. But she's not allowed to call me Cowgirl. Only my mom is.

Aunt Dane is fat, and when she hugs
me she feels like a pillow. She says
I'm too skinny, but my mom is so
skinny you can hardly find her under
her clothes, so I guess that's how some
of us are made. Aunt Dane smells like
whatever she's been cooking.
Sometimes it's apple pie or spaghetti
with garlic sauce. It's different in the
shelter. There you can smell a
thousand smells but most of them
you wish you couldn't.

My bed is hard here too, but it's a good kind of hard, not like you're sleeping on a turtle's back. Aunt Dane says I only have to make my bed on Sundays, but I do it every day. I tuck in the sheets and fluff up my pillows. I make sure the ruffles on my bedspread are all lined up. I keep the good shoes that Aunt Dane bought me under the bed, with the laces undone and a pair of socks already in them, so when my mom comes I'll be ready.

I've got my own room here too, and the only sound I hear is the fish tank. I'm not used to so much quiet. My dreams make a lot of noise. Sometimes it's hard for me to sleep.

Aunt Dane said what I needed was a best friend, so she got Jake. We both hate taking baths, and we're both missing teeth. Aunt Dane got Jake from a family she heard about from one of her friends. Jake's mom had problems too. So we're his foster family now.

For the first few days he wouldn't come when I called, and when I tried to pat him on the head he'd back away. "Jake's got a sack full of memories," Aunt Dane said, "a whole bunch of stuff we don't know anything about. Give him time. Let him unpack."

I wasn't sure what Aunt Dane meant, but she was always saying things like that. When I asked her if Jake's mom was coming back to get him too, she said, "Yesterday is history, tomorrow a mystery. Today is a gift." Aunt Dane says that one a lot.

After awhile Jake started to follow me around and he'd roll on his back so I could scratch his belly. He gets this look in his eyes when he sees me. He tilts his head and perks up his ears. But he still backs away when I reach to pat his head.

Sometimes the three of us sit on the living room rug watching TV. Jake usually falls asleep first. His tail twitches. Aunt Dane snores.

Sometimes I dream that I can't remember exactly what my mom looks like, that I forget she's got warts on one hand and a circle of freckles under her left eye. I wonder what Jake is dreaming about, if he misses his old home, if he'd recognize his mother right away if she came through that door or if he'd have to sniff her real good first. I wonder if Aunt Dane is dreaming that I'm her real daughter or if she's dreaming of a new recipe for super-duper fudge.

Then all of a sudden Jake will lick my face
but I'll pretend to be asleep and Aunt Dane will
carry me into bed. Jake settles into his spot
above my pillow, his paw across my chest.
Aunt Dane tucks me in real gently, like I was a
bird with a broken wing, and kisses my forehead.
I keep my eyes shut the whole time because
I'm afraid if I open them I'll break the spell
and all the good feelings will go away.

"Cowgirl," my mom says. "What day is tomorrow?"

"My birthday!" I shout into the phone.
"Are you coming over?"

"Sure as shootin'," she says. "With a big surprise."

"Remember about Jake," I say.
"Don't pat him on the head."

I bounce on and off the couch. "Whoops, I sat
on a cactus," I say, and ask Aunt Dane if she'll come
out west to visit me on my ranch.

"Can you picture me on a horse?" she asks.

And then I laugh. Aunt Dane likes when I laugh.
She says my laughter is sweeter than the sugar
in her apple pie.

I wake up early and we clean the house.
Jake grabs the broom.

"He knows it's my birthday," I say.
"He wants to help."

I put on my favorite shirt and Aunt Dane braids
my hair. Jake almost lets me tie a bandanna
around his neck. Aunt Dane takes my birthday
cake out of the oven. When it cools, I decorate
the top with frosting and chocolate chips.
We blow up some balloons. Jake grabs the crepe
paper and runs behind the couch.
We turn on the radio.

We wait.

And wait.

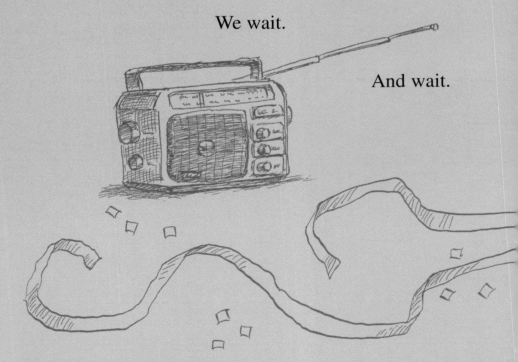

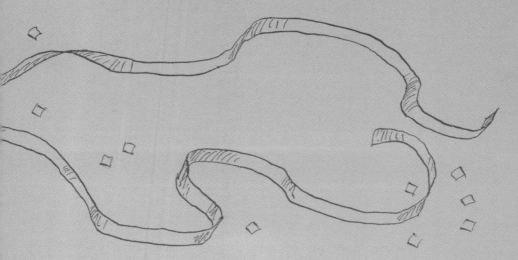

Aunt Dane eats a slice of pizza and then
another, but I'm not hungry. She brings
out some ice cream, but I let mine melt.
Jake falls asleep under my chair.

Aunt Dane calls the place my mom's
supposed to be, then gets out her telephone
book and dials some more numbers,
then shakes her head.

"She's not coming," I say.

"Sorry," Aunt Dane says. "Sorry."
She opens her mouth to say something else,
but scoops me up in her arms instead.
Jake jumps on us too.

"Let's cut the cake. We'll save a piece for your
mom. We'll put it in the freezer and let it sit."

Aunt Dane brings out the cake, but we don't sing and I won't blow out the candles. Aunt Dane closes her eyes and says she'll take care of the wishing part – and the eating part too, and cuts herself a big piece. Aunt Dane hands me a box wrapped up in a bow, but I shake my head. Then she puts it on my lap anyway so I open it up and a knapsack falls out.

"This is from Jake," she says. "It's empty now, but you can fill it up with old stuff, new stuff, whatever you want." She puts another box in my lap. "And this is from me."

"Boots!" I say. "But they're too big. They don't fit."

"They will, " Aunt Dane says. "You'll grow."

Later that night, my mom calls and says
she's sorry Cowgirl, sorry, sorry, she felt sick
but she feels better now, sorry, sorry, sorry,
love you, love you Cowgirl, love you, that she
took a nap and overslept, or maybe she forgot
to set the alarm.

I throw my pillows against the wall,
then my ruffle bedspread. I pull at the sheets.
Jake hides behind a chair.

"Don't give up on me, Cowgirl," mom says in
a voice so soft it makes me stop. "Don't give
up on us."

"Where's my surprise?"

"Right here," she says.

"What is it?"

"You'll see."

"When?"

"Soon. I promise."

Then I give the phone to Aunt Dane because
crying on the phone and letting someone else
see you is even worse than crying by yourself.

"Yesterday is history, tomorrow a mystery,"
I hear Aunt Dane's words in my head. "Today
is a gift." I'm not sure about any of that or
the pot of gold at the end of the rainbow and
the gumdrop trees. I think she made that stuff
up. But the part about life not being fair
sometimes, but still knowing, just knowing,
things were gonna get better, well Aunt Dane
says she's gonna help me hold on to that.

"Every day can be a birthday, why not?"
she says. "It just gives me the chance to bake
another cake."

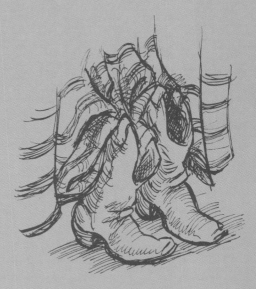

I try to put my new boots under the bed, but they don't fit. I put them in my knapsack instead and hang it from a hook on my closet door. Jake drops his bone at my feet, and I put that in there too.

I reach to pet Jake's head, and this time he doesn't back away! He sits and tilts his face and stares into my eyes. I rub between his ears and down onto his nose. Then he smiles.

"Look, Aunt Dane," I say. "I found the right spot."

Aunt Dane laughs.
Then she hugs me
and this time she
smells like birthday
cake, so I ask her to
cut it up and she
gives herself a slice
and an even bigger
one for me.

Note to Caregivers

by Jennifer Wilgocki, M.S., and Marcia Kahn Wright, Ph.D.

Children who live with caregivers other than their parents can experience a wide range of complicated feelings. *Finding the Right Spot* offers children in placement a chance to think about themselves, their situations, their feelings, and their dilemmas. In addition, adults reading this book may learn to better understand the child's perspective and become alert to the opportunities for conversation that the story offers. (*Note:* For simplicity's sake, we use the term "foster care" throughout this note, but the ideas apply to the many different living arrangements that children find themselves in when they cannot live with their parents.)

The Child's Experience

"She's not coming."

Disappointment. Regardless of the quality of their experience in foster care, disappointment is a feature of the lives of children who have been placed outside their homes. For some children, it is a disappointment simply to be placed in foster care; it means that their parents have not been able to take good enough care of them. For some children, disappointment can come with a missed visit, an unsatisfying phone call, or a broken promise.

Loss. Even if foster care provides relief or a reprieve from abuse, it always involves some kind of loss as well. A child's feelings of loss may be about his or her parents but may also be about siblings, pets, friends, school, or other things. The depth of loss that accompanies out-of-home placement should not be underestimated.

"We wait... And wait."

Uncertainty. Living in foster care involves uncertainty. Children may feel uncertain about how birth parents or siblings are doing. They may feel confused about whether they'll be staying or moving, going to the same school or a different one, having the same friends or needing new ones. And they frequently feel unclear about the long-term plan for their future. Living in the midst of these uncertainties requires courage and help.

"We'll go out west."

Hope. For children in foster care, there is a lot to hope for. They can hope that they will live with their parents again, or that they will stay with their foster family. They hope that when adults make promises, these promises will be kept. As discouraged as they may become, they don't give up hope easily, and it is important to remember that children in foster care are probably hoping for *something*.

"Boots!...They don't fit."
"They will...You'll grow."

There is also a broader hope that we want to cultivate and help children sustain: the hope that rests on belief in themselves and the optimistic feeling that the future will bring good possibilities. Children need to know and believe that their lives will be longer and larger than foster care.

"She's not allowed to call me Cowgirl."

Complicated Loyalties. Children in foster care often feel torn between their biological families and their foster families, regardless of their situation. Loyalty is a powerful aspect of their love for the important people in their lives. They don't automatically understand or believe that it's all right to love many different people at the same time. It often takes a long time and much emotional work for children in foster care to let themselves care about more than one family and not feel a pressure to choose.

What the Caregiver Offers

Listening. One of the most important things a caregiver can offer is the chance to talk and a listening ear. Ideally, children will talk about their own stories, their feelings, their reactions. As a listener, you can make things mentionable and give permission for the child to have many conversations with you. Reading this story provides another opportunity for you to say:
- It's okay to talk about any aspect of foster care and to ask me any question.
- If I don't know the answer, I'll do the best I can to find out.
- It's okay if we don't see things exactly the same way.
- I will try to do a good job listening.
- You can talk about the parts that are sad or bad as well as the good parts.
- You can always talk to me.

"Give him time. Let him unpack."

Pace and Empathy. Children differ in their adjustment to living away from their parents. Each child adjusts at an individual pace, depending on such things as his or her ability to cope with new experiences and information, tolerance for intense feeling, capacity for emotional connection, and ability to receive comfort and to comfort him- or herself. It's important that caregivers strive to follow both the child's lead and the child's pace.

"'Sorry,' Aunt Dane says. 'Sorry.' She opens her mouth to say something else, but scoops me up in her arms instead."

There are many ways for a caregiver to communicate understanding. Sometimes words are best, and caregivers can often help children put their feelings into words. At other times, gestures can be a powerful way to communicate. A hug or smile can show deep empathy without verbalizing things that are too far away from what the child is ready to grasp or manage.

When children have strong feelings, they need their caregivers to be "emotional containers." The caregiver's job is to tolerate, witness, and not be overwhelmed by the child's feelings. The caregiver thus reassures the child and also models how to bear intense feeling without having to shy away, act badly, or fear the experience. Caregivers can also model an ability to tolerate the complexity of the situation without having to brush away or deny the child's feelings. Adults often want to solve or fix the dilemmas and feelings faced by the child. However, we can't resolve every difficulty, and sometimes the most genuine, empathic responses are "I don't know," "I'll try to find out," or simply "I know it's hard."

Managing Your Own Feelings. In addition to bearing the child's feelings, caregivers also have to manage their own. They may have feelings about what happened to the child in the past, about the child's behavior, about the child's current experiences, or many other things. To really listen, caregivers need to find ways to handle their own feelings and reach out for support and consultation as needed.

"She says my laughter is sweeter than the sugar in her apple pie."

The Child's Identity. Part of a caregiver's job is to think of the child as a "child in foster care" rather than a "foster child"—to notice and treasure things about the child that have nothing to do with the circumstances of his or her placement. Caregivers can help children hold on to the knowledge and feeling that who they are is more than a foster child. When children enter foster care, a piece is added to their identity and life experience, but it should not outweigh the other experiences or qualities they bring with them.

Vital Support. The work of caregivers is crucial. They strive to acknowledge the complexities of out-of-home placement, to validate children's feelings, to support their coping, to diminish their aloneness, to lighten their burdens of guilt or confusion, and to provide opportunities for them to speak about their experiences. In this supportive context, children are helped immeasurably to grow and to live full lives.

Jennifer Wilgocki, M.S., and Marcia Kahn Wright, Ph.D., are child and family therapists at the Mental Health Center of Dane County in Madison, Wisconsin. They are the co-authors of Maybe Days: A Book for Children in Foster Care.

About the Author

JANICE LEVY is a former ESL and Spanish teacher, and the author of *Totally Uncool, The Spirit of Tío Fernando, Abuelito Eats with His Fingers,* and *The Man Who Lives in a Hat.* She lives in New York with her husband, two children, and Zoe the Wonder Dog, who always finds the right spot.

About the Illustrator

WHITNEY MARTIN'S illustrations appear in books, magazines, and catalogs, and he has worked on many animation projects, including Walt Disney movies. Before his career as an artist, he was a sergeant in the U.S. Marine Corps Reserves. Whitney now lives in Santa Fe with his wife and two children.